5-Finger Piano Solos With Optional Duet Accompaniments

Selections from

STAR WARS®

Music by JOHN WILLIAMS

Arranged and Edited by Robert Schultz

EXCLUSIVELY DISTRIBUTED BY

HAL•LEONARD®

CONTENTS

From the Twentieth Century-Fox Motion Picture "STAR WARS"

STAR WARS
(Main Theme)

Music by
JOHN WILLIAMS
Arranged by ROBERT SCHULTZ

Accompaniment (*student plays one octave higher*)

Star Wars - 2 - 1
0403B
AS006

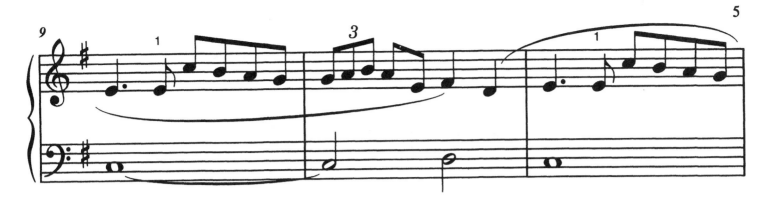

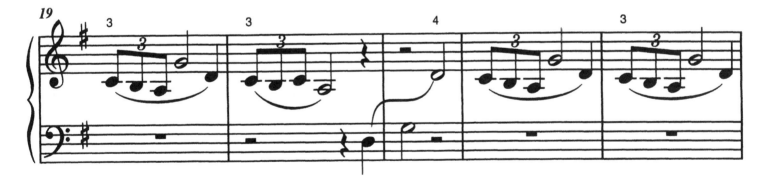

From the Lucasfilm Ltd. Production "STAR WARS" - A Twentieth Century-Fox Release.

CANTINA BAND

Music by
JOHN WILLIAMS
Arranged by ROBERT SCHULTZ

Fast

Accompaniment (*student plays one octave higher*)
Suggested introduction: Play measures 1-2.

Cantina Band - 2 - 1
0403B
AS006

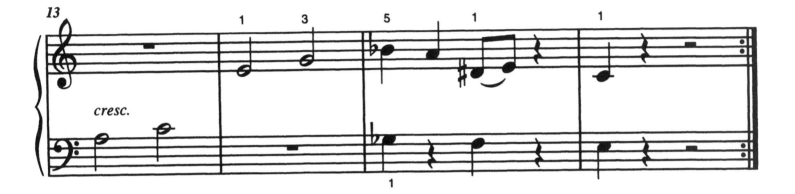

From the Lucasfilm Ltd. Production "STAR WARS" - A Twentieth Century-Fox Release.

PRINCESS LEIA'S THEME

Music by
JOHN WILLIAMS
Arranged by ROBERT SCHULTZ

Accompaniment *(student plays one octave higher)*
Suggested introduction: Play measures 1-2.

Princess Leia's Theme - 2 - 1
0403B
AS006

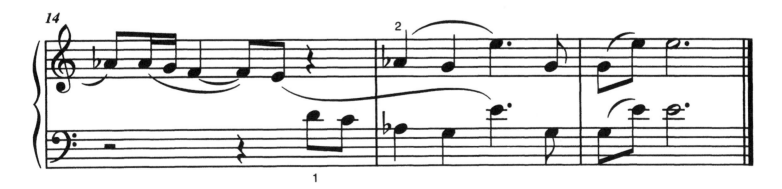

From the Lucasfilm Ltd. Production "THE EMPIRE STRIKES BACK" - A Twentieth Century-Fox Release.

YODA'S THEME

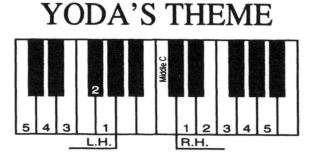

Music by
JOHN WILLIAMS
Arranged by ROBERT SCHULTZ

Accompaniment *(student plays one octave higher)*

Yoda's Theme - 2 - 1
0403B
AS006

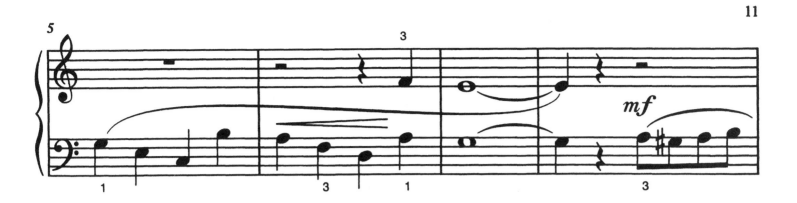

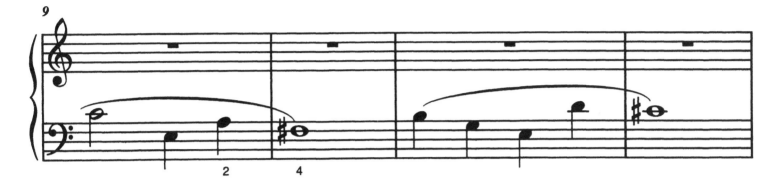

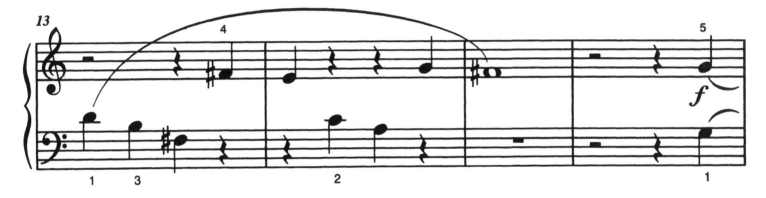

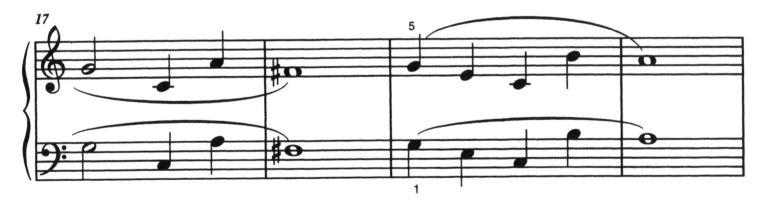

From the Lucasfilm Ltd. Production "THE EMPIRE STRIKES BACK" - A Twentieth Century-Fox Release.

THE IMPERIAL MARCH
(Darth Vader's Theme)

Music by
JOHN WILLIAMS
Arranged by ROBERT SCHULTZ

March

Accompaniment *(student plays one octave higher)*
Suggested introduction: Play measure 1 two times.

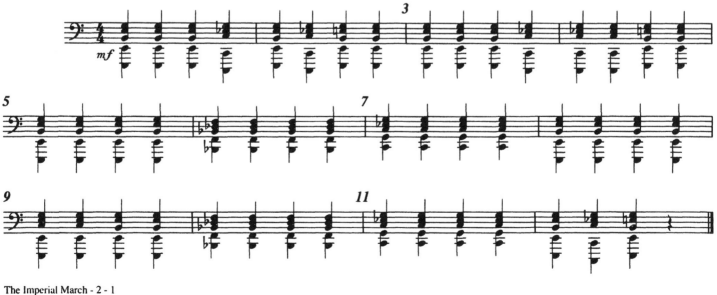

The Imperial March - 2 - 1
0403B
AS006

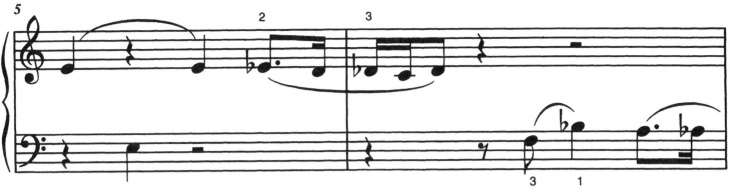

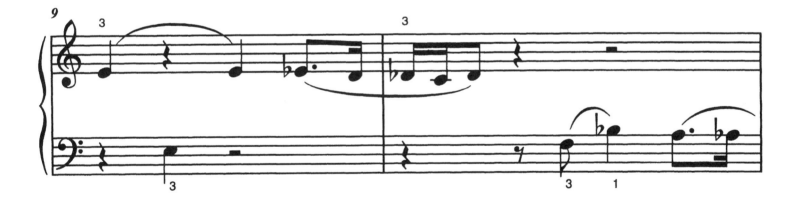

The Imperial March - 2 - 2
0403B

From the Lucasfilm Ltd. Production "RETURN OF THE JEDI" - A Twentieth Century-Fox Release.

LUKE AND LEIA

Music by
JOHN WILLIAMS
Arranged by ROBERT SCHULTZ

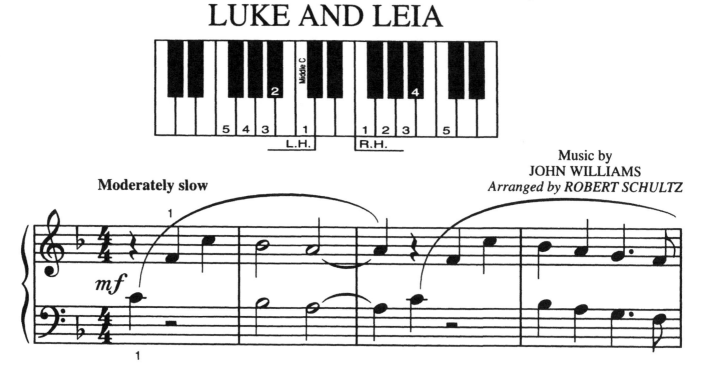

Moderately slow

Accompaniment *(student plays one octave higher)*

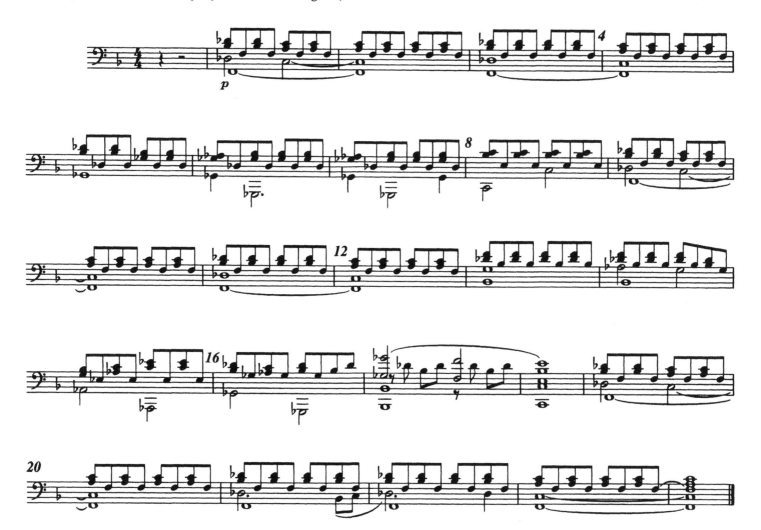

Luke and Leia - 2 - 1
0403B
AS006

From the LUCASFILM LTD. Production "STAR WARS: Episode I The Phantom Menace"

ANAKIN'S THEME

Music by
JOHN WILLIAMS
Arranged by ROBERT SCHULTZ

Moderately

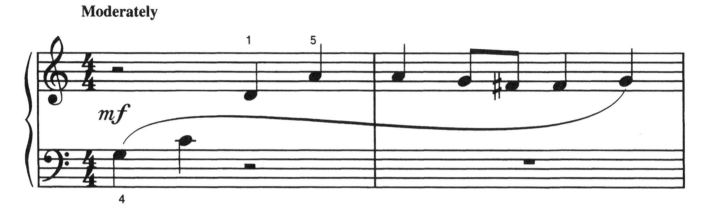

Accompaniment *(student plays one octave higher)*

Anakin's Theme - 2 - 1
0403B
AS006

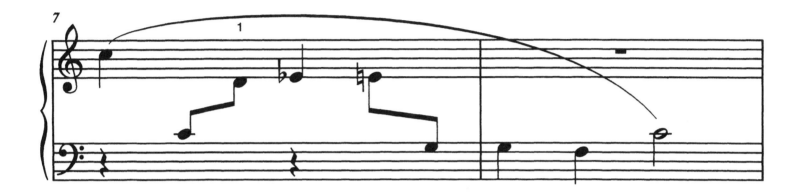

Anakin's Theme - 2 - 2
0403B

From the LUCASFILM LTD. Production "STAR WARS: Episode I The Phantom Menace"

DUEL OF THE FATES

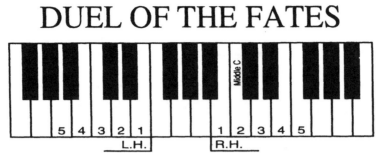

By JOHN WILLIAMS
Arranged by ROBERT SCHULTZ

Accompaniment *(student plays one octave higher)*
Suggested introduction: Play measure 1 two times.

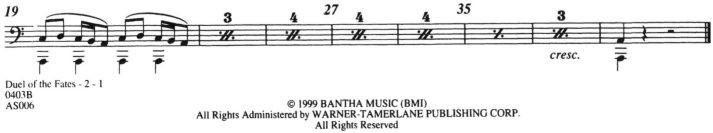

Duel of the Fates - 2 - 1
0403B
AS006

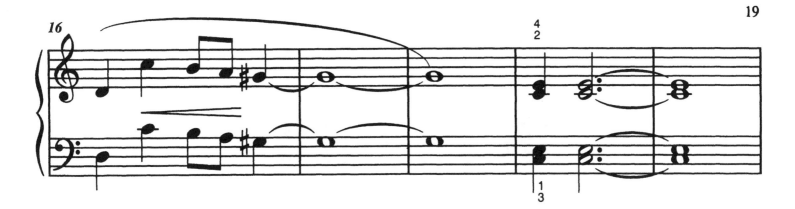

From the LUCASFILM LTD. Production "STAR WARS: Episode I The Phantom Menace"

AUGIE'S GREAT MUNICIPAL BAND

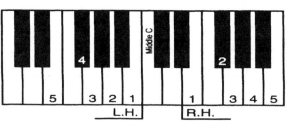

Music by
JOHN WILLIAMS
Arranged by ROBERT SCHULTZ

Joyously

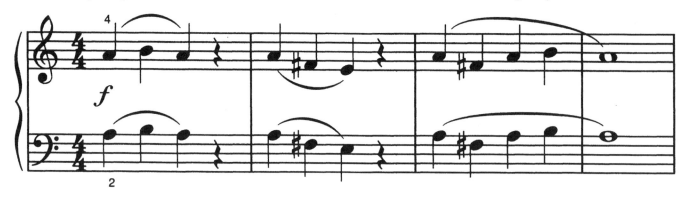

Accompaniment *(student plays one octave higher)*
Suggested introduction: Play measures 11-12.

mf detached

Augie's Great Municipal Band - 2 - 1
0403B
AS006

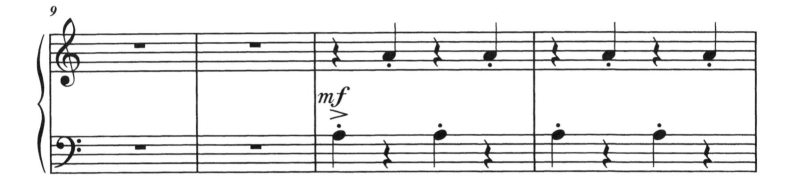